New Orleans Memories

New Orleans Memories

Written and Compiled by Constance Snow

Artwork by Tommy McAfee

TRAVEL MEMORIES PRESS

Indianapolis • Toronto

New Orleans Memories
First Edition

Text © 2001 by Constance Snow
Artwork © 2001 by Tommy McAfee

All rights reserved
ISBN 0-89730-238-9

Publisher: R. J. Berg
Series Editor: Ginny Berg

TRAVEL MEMORIES PRESS
P. O. Box 30225
Indianapolis, IN 46230-0225
Phone 800.638.3909 or 317.251.4640

Printed in Hong Kong

Front cover illustration: Jackson Square and Saint Louis Cathedral
Back cover illustration: French Quarter Carriage Ride

Contents

Illustrations

Acknowledgments

Antoine's

Pamela D. Arceneaux—
    Historic New Orleans Collection

Chef Daniel Bonnot

Brennan's Restaurant

Camellia Grill

Central Grocery

Commander's Palace

Cookin' Cajun Cooking School

Destrehan Plantation

Domilise Bar

French Market

Gumbo Shop

Hotel Maison de Ville and the
    Audubon Cottages

Mother's Restaurant

Mr. B's Bistro

Napoleon House

New Orleans Metropolitan Convention
    and Visitors Bureau

New Orleans School of Cooking

Palm Court Jazz Cafe

Praline Connection Gospel and Blues Hall

Progress Grocery

Restaurant des Familles

Saint Louis Cathedral

Kenneth Snow

Soniat House

Steamboat Natchez

Upperline Restaurant

Priscilla Fleming Vayda

Introduction

New Orleans unveils her charms slowly, leading you along sidewalks shadowed in soft gaslight, through secret gardens, to lacy iron balconies scented by flowering vines. Streetcars rumble beneath overarching oak trees, past antebellum mansions illuminated by crystal chandeliers that glimmer behind lead glass doors. Smoky clubs and coffeehouses vibrate with the howls of jazz cats and blues hounds. Grand Creole restaurants court diners with lavish menus and formal service, while creative young chefs stir up some healthy competition at chic little bistros. Just follow your nose, eyes, and ears. Here, appetites are meant to be indulged.

America's most European city celebrates the senses, from the earthy notes of a street-corner musician to the ethereal aromas of hot baguettes, slow-simmered gumbos, and roasting coffee beans. Shuttered French doors open wide to welcome echoes of a slower time, the clip-clop of horse-drawn carriages or muted foghorns from ships on the river. Medieval traditions of Carnival live on in the wild colors and spirited anarchy of Mardi Gras, while thoroughly modern crowds cheer (and curse) the Saints at the Louisiana Superdome. And during the holidays, a visit to the dazzling Angel Hair Christmas Lobby at the Fairmont Hotel has been a local tradition for generations.

The French Quarter is still the center of attention—about one hundred square blocks of Creole architecture and historic attractions, a virtual living museum that once comprised the entire city. Today New Orleans stretches over nearly two hundred square miles, from Lake Pontchartrain to the Mississippi River, encompassing the stately houses of the Garden District, the convention hotels and riverfront amusements of the Central Business District, the music clubs of Faubourg Marigny, and the Uptown universities.

Life begins after midnight in this moon-worshiping town, where you can dance until dawn and then watch the sun rise over chicory coffee and beignets at Café du Monde. Such liberty has always been a powerful draw for writers and artists. A 1920s New Orleans literary magazine, *The Double Dealer,* published the early works of then-residents William Faulkner, Ernest Hemingway, and Thornton Wilder. On the lam from embezzlement charges in Texas, William Sydney Porter moved to the French Quarter in 1896 and later adopted the pen name O. Henry. The city often served as a backdrop for plays by Tennessee Williams, and it still inspires native novelist Anne Rice, who continues to live and work in the Garden District. Other famous temporary citizens included Mark Twain, F. Scott Fitzgerald, and Truman Capote.

French Impressionist Edgar Degas painted at his uncle's home on Esplanade Avenue during the 1870s. Today some of Degas's works are on display at nearby New Orleans Museum of Art in City Park. Myriad treasures are to be found in the galleries and antiques shops along Royal and Magazine streets. And the Warehouse Arts District is the scene of an ongoing renaissance, as renovated industrial lofts and stylish restaurants have earned the downtown neighborhood a reputation as the SoHo of the South.

Even the cemeteries are filled with happy chatter when tour groups marvel at the gorgeous old tombs and stone angels crowded into these "cities of the dead." In this atmosphere of determined *joie de vivre,* it's just one more reminder to live for today.

The Rich History of New Orleans

One of the oldest cities in the United States, New Orleans was founded in 1718 by French explorer Jean-Baptiste Le Moyne, sieur de Bienville. The site was just a swampy outpost plagued by floods, hurricanes, and yellow fever, but a plan for the town was drawn up that produced what is now called the Vieux Carré (old square) or French Quarter.

Four years later—with a population of about eight hundred—New Orleans was designated capital of Louisiana. The city was controlled by France from 1731 to 1763, when Louis XV ceded New Orleans and "the island on which it stands" to his cousin, Charles III of Spain. France reclaimed the territory briefly in 1800; then Napoléon I transferred it to the United States in the 1803 Louisiana Purchase.

Fire destroyed New Orleans in 1788 and again in 1794, so most buildings in the present-day French Quarter were actually constructed by Spanish colonists. The Old Ursuline Convent (circa 1745) is the only pure example of French colonial architecture that remains.

By 1840, New Orleans was the nation's third largest metropolis, a dynamic port enlivened by steamboat traffic, thriving agricultural markets, opera houses, grand ballrooms, and fine restaurants.

An influx of immigrants in the mid-1800s taxed the resources of the growing city—then the Civil War and Reconstruction took their toll. Railroads replaced steamboats as the preferred mode of transporting goods, and traffic through the port began to dwindle. Yet by the middle of the twentieth century, the port had regained its vitality and the offshore oil boom brought prosperity. Today tourism has become one of the city's most important industries.

HEART OF THE VIEUX CARRÉ

FRENCH MARKET

The nation's oldest continuing market began in the 1700s as an Indian trading post on the Mississippi River. By the early nineteenth century, it was still a wild scene, where servants and housewives carried their shopping baskets each morning, weaving amongst a motley throng of Native Americans, fur traders, bargemen, and buccaneers. Besides the usual produce and caged fowl, the offerings might have included anything from patent medicines to chattering monkeys or parrots straight off the boats. Dentistry was a spectator sport, complete with brass bands (to draw audiences and drown out the wails of patients). Now the lovely colonnaded structure is more civilized, filled with boutiques and restaurants, but open-air stalls still vend fruits and vegetables as well as Carnival masks, handmade jewelry, and other crafts.

Tomato and Goat Cheese Napoleon

Creole tomatoes are locally grown, with a characteristic sweet taste contributed by favorable weather conditions and Mississippi delta soil. The annual Great French Market Tomato Festival celebrates their arrival each June with live music, marching bands, and food booths. French-born New Orleans chef Daniel Bonnot's towering tomato and goat cheese "napoleon" mimics the layered French pastry.

To Prepare Goat Cheese Mixture: In a mixing bowl, combine goat cheese, cream cheese, onion, garlic, and basil; blend thoroughly. Set aside.

To Prepare Black Pepper Vinaigrette: In blender container, combine vinegar, egg yolk, black pepper, and shallot; mix at medium-high speed to blend well, about 20 seconds. Reduce speed to low and, with blender still running, add olive oil in a steady stream until thoroughly blended. Season to taste with salt.

For each serving, spread goat cheese mixture on three tomato slices; then stack the slices to create a layered "napoleon." Top with a dollop of goat cheese mixture. Place on a chilled salad plate and complete the presentation with a drizzle of black pepper vinaigrette. Garnish with chopped basil.

Goat Cheese Mixture

1 pound goat cheese, at room temperature

1 pound cream cheese, at room temperature

1 red onion, finely diced

1 head garlic, roasted and peeled

½ cup minced fresh basil

Black Pepper Vinaigrette

¾ cup rice wine vinegar

1 egg yolk
(coddle yolk, if desired)

2 tablespoons coarsely ground black pepper

1 shallot, diced

1¾ cups olive oil

Salt

6 ripe medium tomatoes, cut into ¼-inch slices (save uneven end slices for another use)

Chopped fresh basil, for garnish

Yield: 6 servings

FRENCH MARKET
FARM FRESH PRODUCE
FRESH GARLIC
FRESH GULF SEAFOOD
YAMS AND POTATOES
LOUISIANA WATERMELO
ANY TIME
WELCOME FRENCH MARKET
GREEN PEPPERS
D'ANJOU PEARS
GRAPES
HOT PEPPERS
ORGANIC PRODUCE
HOME GROWN
FRESH LETTUCE
CREOLE TOMATOES
T. McABEE
©

Tranquil Beauty, Turbulent Past
Saint Louis Cathedral

Consecrated in 1794, Saint Louis Cathedral remains the signature image of New Orleans, glamorized by tales of duels in the back garden, disastrous fires, and hauntings. It's hard to separate church from state in this old Creole colony, where Catholicism has influenced politics, arts, education—and food. Creative seafood dishes certainly helped relieve the sacrifices of meatless Fridays. Sunday brunch resulted from the custom of fasting through breakfast in order to receive communion at morning mass.

Early slaves intermingled Catholic rites with their own African religions to create the exotic rituals known collectively as voodoo. Even the pagan excesses of Carnival are church-related. French for Fat Tuesday, Mardi Gras is the last chance for a spree before Ash Wednesday begins forty days of Lent.

Gumbo Z'Herbes

A vegetarian gumbo made with fresh greens and herbs is traditionally served on Good Friday, when many Catholics still abstain from meat. The dish may include whatever the garden yields—spinach, turnip greens, collards, cabbage, kale, watercress, parsley, beet tops—but legend has it that you'll make a new friend for each different variety of greens that you throw into the pot. This version is from Priscilla Fleming Vayda, a food writer who grew up on Fleming Plantation in Lafitte.

PLACE GREENS IN A LARGE POT with about 4 cups water (or enough water to cover) and simmer over low heat for 30 minutes. Drain, reserving broth; chop greens. Heat oil in a heavy pot; gradually add flour, stirring constantly, and cook to a pale golden color, about 5 minutes. Add green pepper, onion, celery, and green onions. Cook until vegetables are limp, about 5 minutes. Add garlic and reserved cooked greens; simmer for several minutes. Add reserved broth, bay leaf, marjoram, and thyme. Simmer for 2 hours. Just before serving, stir in filé powder. (Do not let gumbo boil after adding filé or it will turn stringy.) Season with salt and pepper. Serve over hot steamed rice in soup bowls. Garnish with chopped parsley.

3 pounds mixed greens, washed well

2 tablespoons vegetable oil

2 tablespoons flour

1 cup chopped green bell pepper

1 cup chopped onion

½ cup chopped celery

¼ cup chopped green onions

2 cloves garlic, minced

1 bay leaf

1 sprig fresh marjoram

1 sprig fresh thyme

2 tablespoons filé powder (see Note)

Salt and pepper to taste

Hot steamed rice

6 tablespoons chopped fresh parsley, for garnish

Yield: 6 to 8 servings

NOTE: Filé is ground sassafras, a thickening agent that also adds a distinctive flavor to gumbo. It can be purchased in many supermarkets and specialty food stores.

The gumbo may be seasoned by salt pork, sausage, ham bones, or ham hocks, added along with the broth. Before serving, remove ham bones or hocks from the gumbo and trim off meat. Return meat to pot and discard bones.

FIT FOR AN EMPEROR
NAPOLEON HOUSE

Back in 1815, when Napoléon I of France was banished to the tiny South Atlantic island of Saint Helena, a group of Louisiana supporters planned a rescue mission. Pirate Jean Lafitte volunteered his ships, and New Orleans mayor Nicholas Girod donated this 1797 building—his own house—which was refitted for the exiled emperor. Napoléon's untimely death in 1821 put an end to their schemes, but the ghost of a good idea lives on at the city's most beloved watering hole. It's a refuge for those who long to flee the clatter and rush of the twenty-first century. Escape into this colonial time warp shielded by ancient sepia walls, a serene courtyard, and soft classical music. Chill out over a Pimm's Cup (gin cooler) garnished with a wedge of cucumber.

Jambalaya

Jambalaya is similar to Spanish paella, with a name that could be traced to the French jambon (ham) or the West African jambe (mixture). Like Louisiana, it's a spicy blend of many cultures, and it's great for parties. Though the rice and seasoning vegetables are standard, you may use any mixture of meats and/or seafood you like, including crawfish, firm fish fillets, ham, pork chops, turkey, or duck. This is the classic version served at Napoleon House.

HEAT OIL in a heavy skillet or Dutch oven with a tight-fitting lid. Add sausage and chicken; sauté over medium heat until lightly browned, about 5 minutes. Add celery, onions, green pepper, and garlic; sauté until wilted, about 5 minutes. Add all remaining ingredients, except shrimp and green onions, in order given. Bring to a boil; then reduce heat to low and add shrimp and green onions. Cover and simmer until liquid is absorbed and rice is tender, about 30 minutes.

Yield: 6 to 8 servings

¼ cup canola oil

1 pound andouille or low-fat spicy smoked sausage, sliced

½ pound cooked chicken, diced

4 stalks celery, chopped

3 medium onions, chopped

1 small green bell pepper, chopped

4 cloves garlic, minced

1 bay leaf

½ teaspoon dried thyme leaves

¼ teaspoon ground allspice

¼ teaspoon cayenne pepper

¼ teaspoon ground cumin

2 cups raw rice

2 cans (12 ounces each) beef broth or 3 cups bouillon

2 cans (14 ounces each) stewed tomatoes

Salt and pepper

2 pounds raw shrimp, peeled and deveined

6 green onions with tops, chopped

WHO'S BEEN SITTING IN YOUR CHAIR?
ANTOINE'S

The oldest restaurant in New Orleans opened for business in 1840, when Antoine Alciatore welcomed the first in a long line of diners that would eventually include hundreds of famous names—Sarah Bernhardt, the Duke and Duchess of Windsor, Charlie Chaplin, Admiral Richard Byrd, Cecil B. DeMille, Mick Jagger . . . The food and service at Antoine's are set in historic dining rooms graced by polished dark woods, tile floors, potted palms, starched white linens, and formally clad waiters. This is the place to feast on a grand scale, from signature Oysters Rockefeller to flaming Baked Alaska. In a world of offbeat ingredients and superstar chefs, Antoine's is one of a handful of traditional New Orleans restaurants—along with Tujague's (established 1856) and Galatoire's (1905)—that remain dedicated to classic French Creole cuisine.

Chicken Rochambeau

Tackle this grand recipe for roast chicken and you'll see why the saucier, who oversees sauces and sautés, is one of the most valued stars of a French Creole kitchen. You might also try the tangy brown Rochambeau sauce with veal or game. The golden hollandaise is luxurious drizzled over poached egg dishes, steamed vegetables, or sautéed fish. Flavored with a reduction of tarragon-scented onions, it is transformed into a glossy béarnaise, a classic accompaniment for steaks and lamb chops.

PREHEAT OVEN to 350°F. Wash and dry the chickens; rub inside and out with salt, pepper, and butter. Place chickens in a shallow baking pan and bake at 350°F for 1½ hours or until completely cooked.

TO PREPARE BROWN ROCHAMBEAU SAUCE: Melt butter in a medium saucepan; add onion and sauté over medium-high heat until onion begins to color, about 5 to 7 minutes. Add flour and cook, stirring constantly, until mixture turns brown, about 10 to 15 minutes. Blend in vinegar; then add sugar. Add chicken stock, salt, and pepper. Simmer for 20 minutes, stirring occasionally. Yield: 2½ cups.

3 whole chickens, 2½ pounds each
Salt and white pepper
½ cup (1 stick) butter, softened

6 slices cooked ham
2 cups Brown Rochambeau Sauce
2 cups Béarnaise Sauce

Brown Rochambeau Sauce

3 tablespoons butter
1 cup chopped onion
3 tablespoons flour
⅓ cup vinegar
2 tablespoons sugar
2 cups chicken stock
Salt and white pepper

Hollandaise Sauce

8 egg yolks

2 tablespoons lemon juice

2 tablespoons tarragon vinegar

2 cups (4 sticks) butter, melted and
kept warm

¾ teaspoon paprika

Salt and cayenne pepper

Béarnaise Sauce

¼ cup minced white onion

2 tablespoons chopped fresh parsley

2 tablespoons minced tarragon leaves

¼ cup tarragon vinegar

1¾ cups warm Hollandaise Sauce

TO PREPARE HOLLANDAISE SAUCE: In a mixing bowl, combine egg yolks, lemon juice, and vinegar; beat until thoroughly blended. Transfer to the top of a double boiler and cook over simmering water, stirring constantly, until mixture thickens, about 5 to 8 minutes. Remove from heat and beat in butter, a small amount at a time. Add paprika, salt, and cayenne pepper; mix well. Keep warm. Yield: 2 cups.

TO PREPARE BÉARNAISE SAUCE: In a saucepan, combine onion, parsley, tarragon, and vinegar; cook over medium-high heat until mixture is reduced by half, about 8 to 10 minutes. Cool slightly; then add hollandaise sauce and blend thoroughly. Yield: 1¾ cups.

When the chickens are fully roasted, split them in half lengthwise and remove the bones. Reduce oven temperature to 180°F. Place chicken halves in oven to keep warm. Place ham slices in a saucepan with brown Rochambeau sauce; simmer several minutes or until ham is heated through.

To serve, place a slice of ham on each serving plate; spoon some of the brown Rochambeau sauce over the ham. Place a chicken half on each slice of ham; top with béarnaise sauce.

Yield: 6 servings

MANGIA!
CENTRAL AND PROGRESS GROCERIES

Everyone knows about the city's French connection, but like other great ports, New Orleans is a melting pot spiced by settlers from Spain, Africa, England, Ireland, Germany, and Asia. The influence of the large Italian community is widespread, from jazz wildman Louis Prima (born in New Orleans) to the first American saint, Mother Cabrini, who founded an orphanage here. The elegant Monteleone is the city's oldest continuously operating hotel, established by former shoemaker Antonio Monteleone in 1886. At Angelo Brocato Ice Cream and Confectionery, the third generation still creates tantalizing fruit ices and gelati. Central and Progress groceries, neighbors for nearly eighty years, are colorful and aromatic Sicilian delis crowded with Mediterranean foodstuffs, spices, and kitchen gear. Their sandwiches are legendary, stacked high on crusty buns as big as hubcaps.

Muffuletta

The muffuletta takes its name from Sicily's round, seeded loaf of bread that was brought here by Italian settlers. Around the turn of the century, several local bakers began stacking the bread with imported meats and cheeses and chopped olive salad to make the massive sandwiches now served by restaurants and sandwich shops all over town, especially Central and Progress groceries.

To Re-Create Progress Grocery's Muffuletta: Stack the bottom half of the bread with a double layer of low-sodium ham and single layers of sliced provolone cheese and Genoa salami. Finish with a generous layer of chopped olive salad, and spread a few spoonfuls of oil from the salad on the other half of the bread before placing it on top. Cut the sandwich into fourths.

For Central Grocery's Muffuletta: Layer the bread with Emmentaler cheese from Switzerland, provolone cheese, Genoa salami, Holland ham, mortadella sausage, and olive salad.

Many New Orleans supermarkets sell muffuletta bread; both Central and Progress make their sandwiches on United brand. You can substitute any seeded Italian loaf with firm body.

Both groceries sell their own olive salads made from old family recipes. (Central claims more than forty spices and other ingredients.) For a good homemade version, begin with a jar of *giardiniera* (Italian-style marinated vegetables)—not too sour—that contains red peppers, carrots, cauliflower, celery, pitted Sicilian olives, and cocktail onions. Drain the vegetables; then add more pitted Sicilian olives, sliced celery, minced garlic, oregano, and olive oil. Chop everything coarsely so it's small enough to stay on the sandwich but large enough so you can taste the individual ingredients.

Courtyards and Gardens

Hidden down dark passageways in the French Quarter or splashed across front lawns of the Garden District, the natural hues of New Orleans never fail to tempt and dazzle. To those who look past the gaudy neon of Bourbon Street, this lustrous old city reveals her true colors, from the cool greens of a lily pond to the hot pink blaze of azaleas in spring.

A glimpse into a private Vieux Carré courtyard, secured by an iron gate, is one of the most tantalizing charms. These romantic sanctuaries may be perfumed by heirloom roses like those at Hermann-Grima Historic House, or they may surprise with medicinal herbs such as chamomile, which is still cultivated in the walled garden at New Orleans Pharmacy Museum. Tables set beneath a canopy of pale purple wisteria add to the sultry ambience of the patio at The Court of Two Sisters, a favorite with visitors. Locals linger over coffee and newspapers in the sunny space behind Croissant d'Or.

Beyond the insular French Quarter, picnickers congregate in wide-open green spaces where generations of families and young lovers have played in the shade. City Park, one of America's oldest and largest public parks, is a fifteen hundred–acre oasis graced by winding lagoons, botanical gardens, and more than thirty thousand trees (including the infamous Dueling Oaks, where gentlemen of an earlier time would settle disputes at dawn with pistols for two and brandy for one).

Even workaday neighborhoods are scented by exotic night-blooming jasmine, sweet olive trees, and gardenias. These and other vintage fragrances are preserved by Bourbon French Parfums and cozy old Hové Parfumeur, where it is still possible for gentlefolk to procure vetiver-scented fans.

MORNING GLORY
BRENNAN'S RESTAURANT

For more than fifty years, the epitome of Creole decadence has been Breakfast at Brennan's, a multicourse feast of elaborate egg dishes and flaming crêpes, plus fine wines from one of the best cellars in town. Sun streams into formal dining rooms surrounding a flagstone patio lavished with fancy ironwork and tropical blooms. The mansion was built in 1795 by Don Vincente Rillieux, great-grandfather of French Impressionist painter Edgar Degas. It was later home to the first bank in the Louisiana Territory (established 1804) and to world chess champion Paul Morphy in the 1850s. Founder Owen Brennan helped put New Orleans on the culinary map, inspiring weekend brunches nationwide and popularizing such local classics as Eggs Sardou and Brennan's own Bananas Foster.

Eggs à la Nouvelle Orléans

Breakfast at Brennan's cracks more than a million eggs every year. This popular specialty is one of the simplest to prepare at home. Just add hot French bread, fresh fruit, and chicory coffee for a rich Creole splurge.

MELT ¼ CUP BUTTER in a medium saucepan. Stir in flour and cook over medium heat for 5 minutes, stirring constantly. Gradually whisk in cream and milk. Reduce heat and simmer, stirring frequently, for 10 minutes or until mixture thickens. Stir in brandy and season with salt and pepper to taste. Remove from heat and keep warm.

¼ cup plus 1 tablespoon butter, divided

¼ cup all-purpose flour

2 cups heavy cream

1 cup milk

1 tablespoon brandy

Salt and white pepper

1 pound lump crabmeat, picked over to remove any pieces of shell or cartilage

8 eggs, poached (see Note)

Melt remaining tablespoon of butter in a medium sauté pan; add crabmeat and cook over medium heat for 1 or 2 minutes, being careful not to break up lumps. Spoon equal portions of crabmeat onto each serving plate; then top with two poached eggs. Spoon cream sauce over eggs and serve.

Yield: 4 servings

NOTE: To poach eggs, combine 6 cups water and 2 cups vinegar in a large saucepan and bring to a low boil. Break an egg into a small cup; then gently drop the egg into boiling water, being careful not to break the yolk. Working quickly, repeat until all the eggs are in the boiling water; then reduce heat and simmer for 3 to 4 minutes, moving eggs several times with a spoon so they will cook evenly. When eggs are firm, remove from simmering water with a slotted spoon and place in a pan filled with cool water. Drain eggs well before serving.

GRANDE DAME OF THE GARDEN DISTRICT
COMMANDER'S PALACE

Superchefs Paul Prudhomme and Emeril Lagasse earned their stars at Commander's Palace before launching triumphant solo careers. Founded by Emile Commander in 1880, the landmark restaurant was acquired in 1974 and steered to national prominence by Ella Brennan (who earlier had helped brother Owen establish Brennan's Restaurant in the French Quarter). The turquoise Victorian mansion, surrounded by the magnificent private homes of the Garden District, at one time enjoyed a reputation of a different sort. During the Roaring Twenties, respectable families dined on the first floor while patrons of an upstairs bordello used a separate entrance around the corner. The much-imitated jazz brunch was born here, but every meal is a special occasion in the tropical courtyard and glass-walled dining rooms, where Old South service still flourishes.

Bread Pudding Soufflé

A signature dish at Commander's Palace, this fancified version of New Orleans's favorite dessert is one of the best. The pudding and sauce may be made in advance, and if you wish, you can serve the pudding as is, without the crown of meringue.

TO PREPARE BREAD PUDDING: Preheat oven to 350°F. Grease an eight-inch square baking pan; set aside. Combine sugar, cinnamon, and nutmeg in a large bowl. Add eggs and beat until smooth; then add cream and blend thoroughly. Add vanilla and bread cubes; mix gently. Allow bread to soak up liquid. Place raisins in greased pan; then pour bread mixture over raisins. Bake at 350°F for 25 to 30 minutes or until pudding is golden brown and firm to the touch. (The texture should be moist, not runny or dry. If a toothpick inserted in the center comes out clean, it is done.) Remove from oven and cool to room temperature.

TO PREPARE WHISKEY SAUCE: Place cream in a small saucepan and bring to a boil over medium heat. Place water and cornstarch in a small bowl or cup and whisk; add to hot cream, whisking to blend. Return mixture to a boil; then reduce heat and simmer for a few seconds, whisking constantly and watching care-

Bread Pudding

¾ cup sugar

1 teaspoon ground cinnamon

Pinch of nutmeg

3 medium eggs

1 cup heavy cream

1 teaspoon vanilla extract

5 cups French bread cubes, cut about
1 inch square (see Note)

⅓ cup raisins

Whiskey Sauce

1 cup heavy cream

1 tablespoon water

1½ teaspoons cornstarch

¼ cup bourbon

3 tablespoons sugar

Meringue

9 medium egg whites

¼ teaspoon cream of tartar

¾ cup sugar

fully so mixture doesn't scorch. Remove from heat. Stir in bourbon and sugar. Taste to be sure sauce has a good bourbon flavor and is sweet enough. Add a bit more bourbon or sugar, if desired. Set aside and cool to room temperature.

To Prepare Meringue: In a large bowl, beat egg whites and cream of tartar until foamy. Add sugar gradually, one tablespoon at a time, and continue beating until mixture is shiny and thick. (Test with a clean spoon. Whites are ready when they stand up stiff—like shaving cream—when you pull out the spoon. Do not overbeat or the whites will break down and the soufflé will not work.)

To Complete Bread Pudding Soufflé: Preheat oven to 350°F. Butter six 6-ounce ramekins; set aside. In a large bowl, break half of the cooled bread pudding into pieces using your hands or a spoon. Gently fold in one fourth of the beaten egg whites, being careful not to overmix. Spoon equal portions of this mixture into buttered ramekins.

Place remaining bread pudding in bowl, break into pieces, and carefully fold in remaining egg whites. Spoon this lighter mixture into the ramekins (soufflés will extend about 1½ inches above rims of ramekins). With a spoon, smooth and shape the top of each soufflé into a dome over ramekin rim. Bake at 350°F for about 20 minutes or until golden brown. Serve immediately. Using a spoon, poke a hole in the top of each soufflé at the table; then pour room-temperature whiskey sauce inside the soufflés.

Yield: 6 servings

Note: New Orleans French bread is airy and tender. If you substitute bread that is too dense, it will soak up all of the custard and the recipe will not work.

A Feast for the Eyes
Upperline Restaurant

Like the home of a favorite eccentric aunt, the Upperline's walls are crowded with a sophisticated collection of Southern folk art and the windows are draped by lace curtains. Owner JoAnn Clevenger usually welcomes her guests at the front door. The bright yellow facade of her 1877 townhouse is splashed with flying wizards painted by international star Martin Laborde, who continues to live and work in New Orleans. Inside you'll discover exuberant creations by other Louisiana masters, from arts diva Zella Funck to primitive prodigy Willie White. A cottage garden lines the sidewalk and dining rooms are warmed by armloads of fresh flowers. Local artists and Uptown aristocrats love the genteel quirkiness and stellar menu that specializes in stylized updates of traditional Southern comfort foods.

Fried Green Tomatoes with Shrimp Rémoulade

A Creole rémoulade is a mustard-based sauce mixed with chilled seafood, usually mounded atop shredded lettuce. In typical uptown/downtown style, the Upperline's version is served on a homey bed of fried green tomatoes.

TO PREPARE CREOLE RÉMOULADE: Combine all ingredients and mix well. Adjust seasonings, if needed. (Rémoulade should be tangy and have a perky taste. Bland, it is not!) Cover and refrigerate. Yield: about 4 cups.

TO PREPARE FRIED GREEN TOMATOES: Pour a thin layer of oil in an iron skillet or heavy sauté pan and place pan over medium heat. Dip each tomato slice in egg wash; then coat with seasoned cornmeal. Place tomato slices in skillet (do not crowd) and cook until golden brown on bottom, about 1½ minutes; turn and brown the other side, about 1½ minutes. (Watch your heat. If it's too high, tomato slices will brown before they are thoroughly cooked.) Remove browned tomato slices from skillet and drain on paper towels.

Creole Rémoulade

1 cup virgin olive oil

1 cup light salad oil

¾ cup Creole mustard or any spicy whole grain mustard

½ cup finely chopped celery

½ cup finely chopped green onion tops

⅓ cup prepared horseradish

¼ cup ketchup

2 tablespoons Tabasco sauce (or more to taste)

2 tablespoons minced fresh parsley

4 teaspoons lemon juice

4 teaspoons Worcestershire sauce

4 teaspoons paprika

4 teaspoons sugar

1 tablespoon grated white onion

2½ teaspoons minced garlic

1½ teaspoons garlic powder

Salt (optional)

Fried Green Tomatoes

Salad oil or very light olive oil

*Green tomatoes (green all the way through),
sliced ½ to ¾ inch thick*

Egg wash (1 egg mixed with 1 cup milk)

Cornmeal seasoned with salt and pepper

For each serving—

*6 or 8 medium shrimp, boiled, peeled,
and chilled*

To serve, place two hot fried green tomato slices next to each other on an individual serving plate. Top each tomato slice with three or four chilled shrimp; then drizzle with 2 tablespoons rémoulade.

NOTE: Rémoulade may be prepared up to three weeks in advance. Cover sauce and store in refrigerator. Shrimp may be boiled, peeled, and chilled a day in advance. Fry green tomatoes just before serving.

ARTS AND FLOWERS
HOTEL MAISON DE VILLE AND THE AUDUBON COTTAGES

Thue to its name, Maison de Ville is an intimate townhouse in the artistic heart of the old city. The circa-1800 residence was converted into an elegant small hotel in the 1940s. Secluded in a separate walled compound, seven Audubon Cottages (circa 1788) with deep roofs and exposed beams are favored by visiting celebrities, from Elizabeth Taylor to Mick Jagger. John James Audubon taught drawing lessons in Cottage 1 while working on Birds of America. *Tennessee Williams completed* Streetcar Named Desire *in Room 9, but sometimes polished his manuscript in the sun-washed courtyard. The hotel's tiny and sedate Parisian-style dining room, known simply as The Bistro, is a landmark of contemporary Creole cuisine. Executive Chef Greg Picolo uses the freshest regional ingredients to create his festive, chic comfort food.*

Arugula Salad with Balsamic Orange and Basil Vinaigrette

Louisiana's first citrus trees were planted in the early 1700s by Jesuit priests, who also introduced citrus fruit to Florida and California. Spanish influences shine in this sunny salad from The Bistro.

To Prepare Vinaigrette Dressing: Place vinegar, orange juice, and garlic in a small saucepan. Cook over high heat until mixture is reduced by one third, about 5 minutes. Remove from heat and cool. Strain liquid (discard garlic) and whisk in mustard. Whisk in oil until well blended. Whisk in salt and pepper to taste; then add basil.

To Assemble Salad: Toss arugula with vinaigrette dressing. (Refrigerate any leftover dressing for up to one week.) Adjust seasonings, if needed. Place arugula on individual serving plates. Top with oranges and olives. Sprinkle with toasted pine nuts and serve immediately.

Vinaigrette Dressing

½ cup balsamic vinegar
¼ cup fresh orange juice
⅛ teaspoon chopped fresh garlic
1 teaspoon Dijon mustard
1 cup extra virgin olive oil
Salt and pepper
6 large leaves basil, minced

Salad

¼ pound (or 3 bunches) fresh arugula leaves
3 oranges, peeled, sectioned, and seeds removed
12 large pitted kalamata olives, cut in half
4 rounded tablespoons toasted pine nuts

Yield: 6 servings

CULTIVATED COMFORTS
SONIAT HOUSE

Like many wealthy planters, Joseph Soniat Dufossat built a townhouse in New Orleans so he could conduct his business in comfort and take advantage of sophisticated city pleasures. In classic Creole fashion, his Vieux Carré residence "turned its back to the street." A broad flagstone carriageway led into the central courtyard, the hub of a plantation in miniature with its cool garden surrounded by the owner's apartments, servants' quarters, kitchen, and stable. A 1983 renovation, which also incorporated a second historic building across the street, transformed his pied-à-terre into one of America's most luxurious small hotels. Just steps from the bustle of Jackson Square, mornings are softened by cathedral bells and breakfast in bed—a simple gift of hot buttermilk biscuits with homemade strawberry preserves and café au lait.

Old-Fashioned Molasses Pecan Pie

3 eggs

1 cup packed brown sugar

½ cup molasses

½ cup light corn syrup

3 tablespoons butter, melted

2 tablespoons rum or bourbon

1 teaspoon vanilla

¼ teaspoon salt

1 cup pecan halves or coarsely chopped pecans

1 9-inch pastry shell, unbaked

*M*olasses is the thick brown syrup separated from raw sugar when the cane is processed. It's a bit strong for modern tastes, so the molasses in this recipe is cut with light corn syrup; however, you may substitute a full measure of either.

PREHEAT OVEN to 350°F. Beat eggs with an electric mixer until blended; then beat in brown sugar, molasses, corn syrup, butter, rum or bourbon, vanilla, and salt. Stir in pecans. Pour into pastry shell and bake at 350°F for 55 to 65 minutes or until knife inserted near center comes out clean. Serve slightly warm or at room temperature.

Yield: 8 servings

River, Bayous, and Swamps

From the beginning, New Orleans has been shaped by water. The Crescent City hugs the curves of the Mississippi River in a boggy cradle wrapped by coastal wetlands and 610 square miles of Lake Pontchartrain. Napoléon I called it Île d'Orléans. To early French settlers, it was known as *le flotant,* the floating land.

Settled well below sea level and flat as a crêpe, the city depends on river levees to hold back the Big Muddy, which actually flows ten to fifteen feet above the city's streets. The grassy banks of the levees make a panoramic runway for joggers and dog walkers, especially in Woldenberg Riverfront Park (where you can even catch a glimpse of exotic underwater life in the Aquarium of the Americas). But nothing beats skyline views from the Canal Street ferry as it skims across one of the world's busiest ports, past a lively parade of barges, freighters, cruise ships, and excursion boats.

The River Road from New Orleans to Baton Rouge is an old trade route that once carried enough sugarcane and cotton to pay for such grand plantation manors as Oak Alley, Nottoway, Houmas House, and Tezcuco. A one-day loop drive also passes Creole cottages, country churches, and graveyards crowded with crumbly whitewashed tombs. Even in town, you're never far from the moody and mysterious beauty of the Louisiana bayou country. Just beyond the moss-draped oaks of City Park, the Bayou Saint John Historic District is a languid waterfront neighborhood graced by antebellum mansions and Victorian cottages. And Audubon Zoo boasts America's only urban swamp, an award-winning exhibit enlivened by Cajun cabins, antique boats, and an assortment of startling indigenous varmints—from common muskrats to rare white alligators.

ROLLIN' ON THE RIVER
STEAMBOAT *NATCHEZ*

The steam sternwheeler Natchez *was launched in 1975, ninth in the line of famed riverboats dating back to 1823, all named for the tribe of Indians native to southern Mississippi. The first* Natchez *carried Marquis de Lafayette on his grand tour of America in 1825. A* Natchez *side-wheeler transported Jefferson Davis to Montgomery, Alabama, in 1861 for his inauguration as president of the Confederacy. In 1870, the* Robert E. Lee *defeated* Natchez VI *in the most famous steamboat race of all time. Today the calliope pipes passengers aboard decks decorated with gingerbread trim and waving flags. The festive scene recalls New Orleans's golden years, when Mark Twain sailed from these very banks. Evening cruises drift past city lights, couples strolling along the levees, and mist-shrouded freighters bound for faraway ports.*

Catfish Courtbouillon

A Louisiana fish courtbouillon is nothing like its French ancestor. Here it's pronounced KOO-bee-yon, and it's simmered in a zesty blend of tomatoes and spices much like a Spanish sauce or Caribbean chowder. In place of the fish, you could use peeled and deveined shrimp to make shrimp Creole, or cubes of boneless skinless chicken for chicken Creole.

WARM OIL in a large saucepan or Dutch oven over medium heat; add onions and sauté until golden brown, about 5 minutes. Add celery, garlic, thyme, oregano, black pepper, cayenne pepper, and bay leaves; continue cooking, stirring constantly, for a minute or two or until garlic is fragrant. Stir in tomatoes, beer, and lemon zest. Bring to a boil; then reduce heat to low, cover, and simmer for 1 hour, stirring occasionally to prevent sticking. (The courtbouillon may be prepared to this point and then refrigerated up to three days.)

Add fish fillets to hot courtbouillon and cook gently over medium heat until fish flakes easily, about 5 to 10 minutes. Adjust seasonings, if needed. Garnish with scallions and parsley and serve immediately with steamed white rice.

Yield: 6 servings

2 tablespoons olive oil

2 medium onions, halved lengthwise and sliced into thin wedges

2 stalks celery, thickly sliced

3 cloves garlic, thinly sliced

½ teaspoon dried thyme leaves

¼ teaspoon dried oregano leaves

¼ teaspoon freshly ground black pepper (or to taste)

⅛ teaspoon cayenne pepper (or to taste)

2 bay leaves

2 cans (14½ ounces each) whole tomatoes with juice, coarsely chopped (4 cups)

12 ounces beer (preferably dark ale) or 1½ cups fish or chicken stock

½ teaspoon freshly grated lemon zest

2 pounds catfish fillets or any firm-fleshed fish such as redfish, red snapper, or grouper

Salt

⅓ cup sliced scallions, white and green parts (for garnish)

2 tablespoons chopped fresh parsley (for garnish)

5 cups steamed white rice

Sweet Life on the River Road
Destrehan Plantation

Tour any of the antebellum mansions along River Road and you're sure to hear tales of gilded carriages, month-long house parties, and ballrooms sprayed with the finest French perfumes. Those were the days when Creole aristocrats lived like feudal princes and the common slang for wealth was "rich as a sugar planter." Destrehan is the oldest plantation manor remaining in the lower Mississippi valley. Built in 1787, the house is a lovely example of French colonial architecture, with wide columns, broad porches, hand-hewn cypress timbers, and a deep West Indies–style roof. The enduring success of Louisiana's sugarcane industry can be traced to Jean Noel Destrehan and his brother-in-law, Jean Etienne Boré (first mayor of New Orleans), who perfected the method for granulating sugar in 1795.

Crabmeat and Cheese Fondue

You may not see silk hoopskirts or brocade waist-coats at your next soirée, but here's a party dish that's rich as a sugar planter. The recipe is from Mr. B's Bistro, a New Orleans restaurant that showcases regional growers.

MELT BUTTER in a heavy-gauge saucepan. Add shallot and cook over medium heat until shallot is translucent, about 2 minutes. Add beer to deglaze, stirring to loosen any browned bits on the bottom of the pan. Add cream and bring to a simmer. Reduce heat to medium-low and gradually add cream cheese, whisking to blend. When cream cheese is completely melted, gradually add cheddar cheese, whisking to blend. When cheddar cheese is completely melted, fold in crabmeat and lemon juice; mix well. Add green onions, salt, and pepper. Transfer to a fondue pot to keep warm. Serve with your favorite dipping ingredients.

1 tablespoon unsalted butter

1 large shallot, minced

4 tablespoons pilsner beer

2 cups heavy cream

1 pound cream cheese, cubed while chilled (let stand at room temperature)

¾ pound mild white cheddar cheese, cubed (about 3 cups)

1 pound jumbo lump crabmeat, picked over to remove any pieces of shell or cartilage

Juice of 2 lemons (about ¼ cup)

½ cup finely chopped green onions

½ teaspoon kosher salt

¼ teaspoon white pepper

Dipping ingredients such as French bread, raw cauliflower, broccoli, or mushrooms

Yield: 12 servings as an appetizer

SWAMP VIEWS AND SWASHBUCKLING HISTORY
RESTAURANT DES FAMILLES

Just thirty minutes south of downtown New Orleans, the cypress-shrouded swamps of Barataria were home base for pirate Jean Lafitte in the early nineteenth century. Here he concealed his armada of one hundred sailing ships and his band of buccaneers. Their descendants still live in tiny fishing communities on the maze of waterways, where the Jean Lafitte National Historical Park maintains miles of trails and boardwalks through the woods and wetlands. Right outside the park, the glass wall at Restaurant des Familles overlooks a shadowy bayou populated by alligators, turtles, egrets, raccoons, deer, and other wildlife. Fresh off the boats, seafood is simmered into authentic gumbos and étouffées. Real adventurers can rent canoes next door to paddle through the cattails and water lilies.

Crawfish or Shrimp Étouffée

For the classic Cajun/Creole dish called étouffée, fresh shellfish or chicken is braised in a rich gravy seasoned with the "holy trinity" of onion, garlic, and bell pepper. This homestyle version is from Restaurant des Familles.

MELT BUTTER in a large saucepan over low heat. Add flour and cook, stirring constantly, until mixture (known as a roux, pronounced ROO) turns medium brown, about 20 minutes. Add onion, green pepper, celery, and garlic; cook for about 15 minutes or until vegetables are tender. Add crawfish tails or shrimp (or chicken), lemon juice, salt, black pepper, and cayenne pepper; mix well. Add 1 cup stock or water and bring to a boil; then reduce heat and simmer for 15 minutes. Add green onions and parsley; then gradually stir in remaining 2 cups stock or water to make the gravy. Simmer 20 minutes longer. Serve over hot steamed rice.

6 tablespoons butter
¼ cup flour
1½ cups chopped onion
½ cup chopped green bell pepper
½ cup chopped celery
1 tablespoon minced garlic
1 pound crawfish tails or shrimp, peeled and deveined, or diced boneless chicken
1 teaspoon lemon juice
1 teaspoon salt
¼ teaspoon black pepper
¼ teaspoon cayenne pepper
3 cups stock or water, divided
¼ cup sliced green onions
1 tablespoon minced fresh parsley
Hot steamed rice

Yield: 4 servings

BAYOU COOKING, CITY STYLE

GUMBO SHOP

Local audiences laugh out loud when movies portray New Orleanians speaking with a Cajun accent. That belongs in the country around Lafayette, where French Acadians immigrated from Canada. New Orleans was settled by Creoles, Louisiana-born offspring of European colonials. Much of the confusion comes from the regional cuisine, as many dishes have crossed back and forth between the two cultures. Cajun stews and étouffées began as hearty farm food. Sophisticated Creole sauces and spicy gumbos were stirred up in the metropolitan melting pot by French, Spanish, and African cooks. Gumbo Shop has been a French Quarter landmark since the 1940s, dishing out Creole/Cajun standards in a 1795 townhouse with historic wall murals, antique furnishings, and a tropical courtyard shaded by banana trees.

Seafood Okra Gumbo

Gumbo is the African name for okra, though the odd little pods are not always found in Louisiana's signature dish. Every Cajun/Creole family has its own special recipe for gumbo, but this one is the best-seller at the Gumbo Shop in the French Quarter.

PEEL AND DEVEIN SHRIMP; place shrimp in a covered dish and refrigerate. Rinse shrimp shells and heads; then place in a nonreactive stockpot (such as stainless steel, porcelain, or glass) with 2 quarts water. Bring to a boil; then reduce heat and simmer for 30 to 45 minutes. Strain, discard solids, and reserve stock.

Meanwhile, wash crabs well under running water and place in a nonreactive pot with 1 quart water. Bring to a boil; then reduce heat and simmer for 20 to 30 minutes. Strain, reserving stock and crabs. When crabs are cool enough to handle, snap off both claws and break body in half; set aside.

Heat 2 tablespoons oil in a heavy skillet; add okra and sauté over medium-high heat for about 10 to 15 minutes or until all "ropiness" is gone. (This may take longer for fresh okra.) Remove from heat and keep warm. Heat remaining ⅔ cup oil in a large (eight-quart), heavy, nonreactive Dutch oven over medium-high heat. Add flour to make a roux and cook, whisking constantly, from 5 to 15 minutes. When the roux turns

2 pounds small shrimp, heads on (fresh or frozen, about 40 to 50 per pound)

2 small blue crabs, cleaned (fresh or frozen)

2 tablespoons plus ⅔ cup vegetable oil, divided

1 quart okra, cut into ½-inch rounds (fresh or frozen)

½ cup all-purpose flour

2 cups chopped onion

1 cup chopped green bell pepper

½ cup chopped celery

2 teaspoons minced garlic

1 can (16 ounces) chopped tomatoes

2 bay leaves

2 teaspoons salt (or to taste)

½ teaspoon black pepper

½ teaspoon white pepper

¼ teaspoon cayenne pepper

Hot steamed rice

dark brown, add onion, green pepper, celery, and garlic. Sauté, stirring occasionally, until vegetables are tender. (During this process, allow vegetables to stick to the bottom of the pan a bit; then scrape pan with a metal spoon or spatula. This caramelizes the natural sugars in the onion, giving greater depth of flavor.)

Add tomatoes, bay leaves, salt, and peppers. Cook for about 10 minutes, repeating the stick-and-scrape process with the tomatoes. Add sautéed okra and cook 10 minutes longer. Add crab stock and half of the shrimp stock and bring to a boil, stirring constantly. Reduce heat, partially cover pan, and simmer for about 1 hour, stirring occasionally. If gumbo appears too thick, add a bit more stock. Adjust seasonings, if needed. Add broken crabs and simmer for about 10 minutes. Add peeled shrimp and return to a boil; then reduce heat and simmer until shrimp are firm and pink, about 5 minutes. Remove pot from heat.

As is the case with most gumbos, this dish is best prepared several hours before serving—or even the day before—allowing time for the flavors to marry. When reheating, stir often and take care not to overcook the shrimp. Serve over hot steamed rice in large bowls.

Yield: 8 servings

JUST AROUND THE BEND

CAMELLIA GRILL

Travel back in time at this white-columned diner under the oaks, an Uptown favorite since the doors first opened in 1946. Little has changed since then. Guests still slide onto chrome stools at the gleaming counter, pies are still made from scratch, and the walls are still decorated with vintage floral prints. Snappy service from waiters clad in crisp white linen jackets is reminiscent of an old railroad dining car. On weekends, lines sometimes stretch around the corner, with regular patrons reading the morning paper and chatting amiably in anticipation of the buttery grits, omelets, and pecan waffles to come. Tucked into a curve of the Mississippi, the surrounding Riverbend neighborhood is a lively enclave of fashionable shops, fine restaurants, and student hangouts.

Those Famous Camellia Grill Omelets

*I*f you want to play Dagwood with a spatula, the Chef's Special Omelet at Camellia Grill is stuffed with bacon, ham, potatoes, onions, and Swiss and American cheeses; then it's ladled with chili for good measure. However, amateurs should probably start with something a bit less ambitious.

Camellia Grill's high-rising omelets don't work as well in a skillet, but if you're lucky enough to have a stove with a built-in grill (or a cast iron griddle that fits over one or two burners), here's the secret from one of the veteran cooks:

HEAT THE GRILL, grease it lightly, and scatter on ham, sausage, onions, peppers—whatever fillings you choose. Whip two eggs in a blender until they're light yellow and full of air; then pour them over the other ingredients on the hot grill. Let the eggs cook until they're foaming on top. Add cheese if you wish; then fold the omelet over and roll it onto a warm plate.

Simple Pleasures in the Big Easy

The City That Care Forgot is no place for clock-watchers or calorie counters, as late nights and great eats are bound to tempt the righteous. Jazz fanatics can club-hop until the wee hours and foodies can find a feast at the humblest sandwich shop—and you don't have to be a Rockefeller to let the good times roll. As anyone here will tell you, the best things in life are cheap. These excesses are tempered by a delicious local custom—closing the shutters for a languid afternoon nap. Everybody wakes up with brighter eyes, adjusted attitudes, and one question on their minds: What's on for tonight?

International audiences crowd into Snug Harbor Jazz Bistro when Ellis Marsalis sits down at the piano. Pete Fountain headlines at his own cabaret in the New Orleans

Hilton (and leads his merry Half-Fast Walking Club through the streets every Mardi Gras morning). Football fans sing rah-rah songs on the patio at Pat O'Brien's. And thousands of music lovers dance from stage to stage at the annual New Orleans Jazz and Heritage Festival, soaking up hot sun and cool sounds, from African drums to zydeco.

Café du Monde, still the traditional last stop after a night on the town, has been open 24-7 since the 1860s. Its sidewalk tables across from Jackson Square overlook the moon-splashed spires of Saint Louis Cathedral, a dreamy backdrop for dark chicory coffee (smoothed by steaming milk) and pillow-shaped beignets draped in a cloud of powdered sugar. Let your mind be lulled by a lone saxophonist blowing blue notes on the levee, as you muse on your plans for tomorrow.

AIN'T MISBEHAVIN'
PALM COURT JAZZ CAFE

For more than forty years, devotees have lined up at the "living museum" known as Preservation Hall, crowding onto hard benches to watch performances by legendary masters of traditional jazz. It's a unique and fascinating experience, but many of the same musicians also play a few blocks away in the comfort of the Palm Court Jazz Cafe. This cool oasis recaptures the spirit of the 1920s nightspots where Jelly Roll Morton first pounded out "Midnight Mama" and "Tom Cat Blues." The lofty old French Quarter storefront is fitted with an antique mahogany bar, mosaic tile floors, ceiling fans, and potted tropical plants. Real jazz hounds can fill a doggy bag with takeout music from the adjoining shop, which stocks rare labels such as Audiophile and GHB.

Red Beans and Rice

1 pound dried red kidney beans

2 tablespoons olive or vegetable oil

1 large onion, chopped

1 stalk celery, chopped

2 cloves garlic, minced

¼ teaspoon dried thyme leaves

1 bay leaf

1 meaty ham bone (optional)

1 teaspoon hot sauce such as Tabasco
(or more to taste)

Salt and black pepper

5 cups steamed white rice

Louis Armstrong signed his correspondence "Red beans and ricely yours," and this ultimate comfort food is still the traditional Monday meal for Louisiana families. It's a holdover from the days when homemakers would boil the water for their laundry at the same time.

RINSE AND SORT BEANS (sometimes you'll find tiny rocks); then place beans in a large pot and add enough cold water to cover by two inches. Set aside to soak for at least 3 hours, or refrigerate overnight. Drain.

In a large saucepan or Dutch oven, warm oil over medium heat; add onion and sauté until golden brown, about 5 minutes. Add celery, garlic, thyme, and bay leaf; cook for a minute or two longer or until garlic is fragrant. Add drained beans, ham bone (if desired), and hot sauce; add 6 cups water and bring to a boil. Reduce heat to low, cover, and simmer for about 2½ to 3 hours or until beans are tender, stirring often to prevent sticking. If necessary, add extra hot water (never cold water). For creamiest results, cook the beans a day ahead and refrigerate overnight; then reheat. Adjust seasonings, if needed, and serve over steamed rice with extra hot sauce for those who like it.

Yield: 6 servings

FOOD FOR THE SOUL
PRALINE CONNECTION GOSPEL AND BLUES HALL

Most French Quarter praline shops are plastered with vintage images of women ladling the sugary hot pecans from iron kettles onto marble slabs. For many, it was a ticket to independence in an old world that offered few opportunities for female or minority entrepreneurs. During the 1980s, the Moore and Kaigler families expanded their homemade candy business into the original Praline Connection restaurant in Faubourg Marigny, plus this Warehouse District spin-off that also features live music. The regular menu is pure Creole soul food, and the Sunday gospel brunch is a foot-stomping, rafter-raising invitation to repent your sins (except gluttony). After dark, top local performers sing the blues in this former steamboat factory, which boasts an antique bar that was shipped downriver from a Chicago speakeasy once owned by Al Capone.

Pecan Pralines

1½ cups pecans, preferably roasted
(see Note)

1½ cups sugar

¾ cup packed light brown sugar

½ cup milk

6 tablespoons butter

1 teaspoon vanilla

The Praline Connection's recipe is a family secret, but here's a good one from New Orleans School of Cooking, which has presented Cajun/Creole cooking classes daily in the French Quarter for more than twenty years.

IN A LARGE POT, combine pecans, sugar, brown sugar, milk, and butter. Bring to a boil over medium heat and cook, stirring constantly, until mixture reaches soft-ball stage (238°F to 240°F on a candy thermometer). Remove from heat and add vanilla. Stir until mixture thickens, becoming creamy and cloudy, and pecans stay suspended in the mixture, about 3 to 5 minutes. Drop spoonfuls of the hot mixture onto buttered waxed paper (with a newspaper underneath to absorb the heat), aluminum foil, or parchment paper. Let sit until cool.

Yield: about 30 pralines

NOTE: To roast pecans, spread shelled nuts on a baking sheet. Place in 275°F oven for about 20 to 25 minutes or until slightly browned and fragrant. Watch carefully so they don't burn.

No Shirt, No Shoes, No Service
Neighborhood Restaurants

Ask ten people to name the best neighborhood restaurant in town and you'll get ten different answers. Generations of New Orleanians have bellied up for fried seafood and po-boys at frowzy old hangouts such as Domilise's, Mandina's, Mother's, and Rocky and Carlo's. Liuzza's is typical of the breed, with its funky 1940s decor, neon signs, career waitresses, and draft beer in frozen fishbowl mugs. Mounds of spaghetti and meatballs are slathered with thick red sauce that has simmered for hours. Platters are piled high with soft-shell crabs or jumbo shrimp in a crackly golden crust of seasoned cornmeal. Every seat is taken (and filled to its capacity). This is the place to get an earful of local gossip, unsolicited political opinions, and authentic N'Awlins accent.

Po-boys

The king of New Orleans's sandwiches was created during a 1920s streetcar strike by former conductors Bennie and Clovis Martin, who promised to feed all union members for free. Whenever a striker entered their sandwich shop, Bennie would yell to Clovis, "Here comes another poor boy!"

Fried Shrimp or Oyster Po-boy

The third generation operates Domilise Bar on Annunciation Street, where Peter and Sophie Domilise first began serving po-boys to longshoremen from the nearby riverfront some seventy years ago.

"Peel the shrimp and soak them in beaten egg seasoned with salt, pepper, and Zatarain's Creole seasoning," says Patti Domilise, who cooks the seafood for the po-boys. "Roll the shrimp in corn flour [finely ground cornmeal] with salt and pepper; then deep-fry just until they turn golden brown and float. We set the big fryer at the restaurant between 340 and 350 degrees, but I set my Fry Daddy at home a little higher. It's the same for oysters, but skip the egg wash. Just roll them in the corn flour."

To make a seafood po-boy, Patti piles shrimp or oysters on French bread with mayonnaise, lettuce, pickle slices, ketchup, and hot sauce.

Roast Beef Po-boy

Mother's Restaurant has been a landmark on Poydras Street since 1938. At the restaurant, owner Jerry Amato uses whole rounds of beef, but for home kitchens, he recommends a much smaller cut of top round. Season the roast to taste with salt, pepper, thyme, and garlic. Place it in a large pan with enough beef stock to come halfway up the roast; then surround it with whole garlic cloves, onions, celery stalks, and carrots. Cover pan and braise roast in a 300°F oven until the meat is tender enough to shred along the bottom [about 40 to 50 minutes per pound, depending on the quality of the meat]. Strain out the vegetables, but be sure to save all of the "debris" (beef shreds and gravy).

To make a roast beef po-boy, split French bread and spread bottom half with brown mustard, mayonnaise, sliced beef, and shredded cabbage. Slather the other half with debris and place it on top.

Hot Boiled Crabs and Spicy Heritage
Lakefront Seafood Restaurants

Before air conditioning, folks escaped the city heat by heading out to West End Park for cool breezes and shady pursuits at the historic seafood houses that stand on pilings over Lake Pontchartrain. Flappers guzzled bootleg hooch and danced on the bars here during Prohibition. Illegal slot machines clanged throughout the '30s and '40s. Today the waterfront decks and screened dining porches are still a major destination for those in search of seafood in a casual family atmosphere. Weekend sailors dock out back for dinner. Amateur athletes dive for balls at the sand volleyball courts. A footbridge across the 17th Street Canal leads to the picturesque fishing harbor of Bucktown, with its colorful strand of shrimp boats and fishing camps, plus another cluster of deliciously downscale eateries.

New Orleans Seafood Boil

Louisiana's answer to a clambake is traditionally cooked outdoors for large parties. This smaller recipe is adjusted for a kitchen stove, but it could be halved or multiplied. The traditional seasonings add lots of flavor without overpowering the fresh taste of the crabs and shrimp. If you prefer an extra-hot whammy, just increase the amount of cayenne and black peppercorns. Most cooks throw a little something extra into the pot, such as smoked or Italian sausages, whole trimmed artichokes, cauliflower heads, and/or fresh mushrooms.

COMBINE ALL SEASONINGS and tie securely in a cheesecloth bag. Place seasoning bag in a canning pot or large stockpot with 2 gallons water; add onions, lemons, celery, garlic, salt, and cayenne pepper. Bring to a rolling boil; then reduce heat, cover, and simmer for 20 minutes.

Add the rest of the ingredients in the following order, letting the liquid return to a boil after each addition before timing: Add potatoes and boil for 5 minutes; add crabs and boil for 10 minutes; add corn and boil for 10 minutes; add shrimp and boil for 2 minutes. Turn off heat and let ingredients steep in broth for 10 minutes. (This entire process should take about 35 to 40 minutes.)

Yield: 4 to 6 servings

Seasonings

⅓ cup coarsely chopped fresh gingerroot

10 bay leaves, crumbled

2 tablespoons fennel seeds

2 tablespoons mustard seeds

2 tablespoons whole peppercorns
(or more to taste)

1 tablespoon whole allspice

1 tablespoon whole cloves

Seafood Boil

6 medium onions, whole and unpeeled

2 lemons, quartered

2 stalks celery with leaves, cut into thirds

1 head garlic, quartered and unpeeled

¾ cup salt

1 tablespoon ground cayenne pepper
(or to taste)

3 pounds small new potatoes,
unpeeled and scrubbed

24 live crabs

6 ears fresh corn, shucked and broken in half

5 pounds shrimp, heads on and unpeeled

HISTORY ON THE HALF-SHELL
OYSTER HOUSES

"He was a bold man that first eat an oyster," Jonathan Swift observed, and the great old oyster bars of New Orleans do maintain a distinctly macho atmosphere. Businessmen stand shoulder to shoulder at the counter, downing a quick dozen for lunch. Facing the customers across heaps of crushed ice, a shucker works furiously, balancing each shell in a rubber mitt as he pries it apart with an evil-looking curved knife. Louisiana writer James Lee Burke mentions The Pearl in his detective novels, while other local experts swear by Casamento's or The Acme. Some like their oysters fried, or broiled in garlic butter, or simmered into creamy stews. But real aficionados just add a squeeze of lemon and a shake of Tabasco; then they slurp the still-living bivalves right off the half-shells.

Oyster Artichoke Soup

Cookin' Cajun Cooking School welcomes more than twenty thousand students each year to its daily cooking seminars in Riverwalk's Creole Delicacies gourmet shop. This is one of owner Lisette Verlander's favorite recipes, a family tradition to serve at Christmas parties.

TO COOK FRESH ARTICHOKES, bring a large pot of salted water to a boil; add vinegar. Add fresh artichokes and cook over medium heat for 45 to 55 minutes or until tender. Drain and cool. Scrape leaves and chop hearts. If using canned artichoke hearts, just chop the artichokes. Set aside.

Melt butter in a large Dutch oven over medium heat. Add oil and flour and cook, stirring constantly, until flour is browned, about 5 minutes. Add green onions, onion, and celery. Sauté for 15 minutes, stirring often. Add reserved artichoke scrapings and hearts, turkey or chicken stock, ham, parsley, garlic, seasoned salt, and pepper. Simmer for 20 minutes.

In another pan, heat oysters and their liquor until edges of the oysters curl, about 3 minutes. Drain liquid into soup mixture. Cut up oysters and add to soup. (If oysters are small, you can leave them whole.) Simmer 15 minutes longer. Adjust seasonings, if needed.

Yield: 12 servings

5 medium artichokes or 3 cans
(16 ounces each) artichoke hearts, drained

Salt

1 tablespoon vinegar

½ cup (1 stick) butter

1 tablespoon vegetable oil

¼ cup flour

1 bunch green onions, chopped

1 cup chopped onion

½ cup chopped celery

1 quart turkey or chicken stock

4 ounces lean ham, chopped

2 teaspoons chopped fresh parsley

1 clove garlic, chopped

1 tablespoon seasoned salt (or more to taste)

1 teaspoon black pepper

5 dozen oysters, with their liquor

New Orleans Historical Timeline

1400s — The region that would later be known as Louisiana is inhabited by Native American tribes, including the Atakapa, Caddo, Chitimacha, Muskogean, Natchez, and Tunica.

1519 — Spanish explorer Alonso Álvarez de Pineda reports sighting the mouth of a great river, probably the Mississippi.

1541 — Hernando de Soto claims portions of present-day Louisiana for Spain, planting the first of ten different flags that would fly over the state.

1682 — Robert Cavelier, sieur de La Salle, claims the entire Mississippi valley for France and names it Louisiana for King Louis XIV.

1718 — Jean-Baptiste Le Moyne, sieur de Bienville, establishes New Orleans and names it for the French regent, Philippe, duc d'Orléans.

1722 — The capital of Louisiana is moved from Biloxi to New Orleans.

1731 — Louisiana becomes a French crown colony.

1762–3 — France's Louis XV cedes New Orleans and "the island on which it stands," plus all of Louisiana west of the Mississippi River, to his cousin, Charles III of Spain. The transfer is confirmed by the Treaty of Paris, which also grants England title to property east of the Mississippi.

1764–88 — French Acadians, expelled from Canada by British forces, establish the earliest Cajun communities in southwestern Louisiana.

1788 — Much of New Orleans is destroyed by a major conflagration, followed by another disastrous fire in 1794.

1789 — A number of aristocrats and royalists from France arrive in New Orleans after fleeing the French Revolution.

1791 — Refugees from an insurrection in Santo Domingo arrive in New Orleans.

1800–1	Spain secretly cedes Louisiana back to France. The transfer is confirmed by the Treaty of San Ildefonso.
1803	The Louisiana Purchase is approved by President Thomas Jefferson, and Napoléon I sells the territory to the United States for $15 million—about three cents per acre.
1805	New Orleans is incorporated as a municipality. Americans settle upriver from the French Quarter in a suburb called Faubourg Sainte-Marie, which evolves into the central business district of the city.
1812	Louisiana is the eighteenth state to join the Union. The *New Orleans,* the first steamboat to navigate the Mississippi River, arrives in New Orleans, where port traffic and agricultural commerce thrive.
1815	At the conclusion of the War of 1812, General Andrew Jackson's army successfully defends the city against British invasion in the Battle of New Orleans.
1838	The first official Mardi Gras celebration takes to the streets in New Orleans.
1853	The worst in a series of yellow fever epidemics claims more than eight thousand lives in New Orleans.
1861	Louisiana secedes from the Union, operating as an independent republic for six weeks before joining the Confederacy.
1862	New Orleans falls to Union forces during the Civil War.
1868	Louisiana is readmitted to the Union with a new state constitution that grants voting rights to African-Americans.
1877	President Rutherford B. Hayes withdraws federal forces from Louisiana, ending the political and social turmoil of Reconstruction.
1879	Construction of jetties forces the Mississippi River to cut a deeper channel, allowing ocean-going vessels to sail upriver.
1897	In an effort to restrain widespread prostitution, a thirty-eight-block area of New Orleans is designated where brothels and saloons can operate. The district is known as Storyville, adopting the name of Sidney Story, the city alderman who got the ordinance passed.

Late 1800s– early 1900s	A type of improvised music is inspired by the syncopated sound of ragtime that jangles through New Orleans's backstreets and bordellos. Finally recognized as a distinctive art form, this music is named jazz.
1917	After years of decline, the Storyville district is closed down when the United States enters World War I. The army and navy prohibit prostitution within five miles of military sites.
1938	Tennessee Williams arrives, beginning a long career associated with New Orleans, the background for many of his plays.
1960	Racial integration of public schools begins.
1970	The first New Orleans Jazz and Heritage Festival is held in Beauregard Square (now known as Congo Square), attracting a handful of spectators. The current celebration rivals Mardi Gras as a magnet for tourism.
1975	The Louisiana Superdome is completed in downtown New Orleans at a cost of more than $163 million.
1977	Ernest N. "Dutch" Morial is the first African-American to be elected mayor of New Orleans.
1991	Riverboat gambling is legalized in Louisiana.
1997	New Orleans hosts the Super Bowl for the eighth time—more than any other city (until Miami hosts its eighth Super Bowl in 1999).

New Orleans Memories / 67

Annual Events in the New Orleans Area

January   Nokia Sugar Bowl / Carnival season opens on Twelfth Night (January 6) / Battle of New Orleans reenactment at Chalmette Battlefield

February–March   Carnival season closes with Mardi Gras (the "Fat Tuesday" before Ash Wednesday) / Celebrations for St. Patrick's Day (honoring the patron saint of Ireland) and St. Joseph's Day (observing a tradition introduced by Sicilian immigrants) / The Tennessee Williams New Orleans Literary Festival

April–May   French Quarter Festival / New Orleans Jazz and Heritage Festival

June   Great French Market Tomato Festival / Reggae Riddums International Arts Festival

July   Go 4th on the River / New Orleans Wine and Food Experience

August   White Linen Night in the Warehouse Arts District / Blessing of the shrimp fleets in St. Bernard Parish

October   Louisiana Swamp Fest at Audubon Zoo / Art for Arts' Sake at the Contemporary Arts Center / Gumbo Festival in Bridge City / Ghostly Gallivant in the French Quarter

November   All Saints' Day (November 1) / Destrehan Plantation Fall Festival / Bayou Classic football game between Grambling and Southern universities

December   A month-long festival of events celebrates Christmas, New Orleans Style! / New Year's Eve celebrations

For more information about these and other events in the greater New Orleans area, contact:

*New Orleans Metropolitan Convention and
   Visitors Bureau
1520 Sugar Bowl Drive
New Orleans, LA 70112-1259
Phone – 504.566.5003 or 800.672.6124
Fax – 504.566.5046
Internet – www.neworleanscvb.com*

Index